MR. WEBSTER IN HIS LETTERS.

By
E. D. Sanborn

PROF. E. D. SANBORN, LL. D.

DEAR SIR,

In accordance with a vote of the Senior Class, the undersigned Committee present thanks for your able and eloquent Lecture upon DANIEL WEBSTER, and request the favor of a copy for publication. The above request is not offered as a mere compliment; but is dictated by our desire to preserve, in a more permanent form, the presentation of a subject so interesting to all.

Yours, respectfully,

JAMES POWELL,
WALDEMER OTIS,
HENRY C. IDE.

HANOVER, Nov. 14, 1865.

HANOVER, Nov. 15, 1865.

MESSRS. POWELL, OTIS AND IDE,

The Lecture which the Senior Class so kindly solicit for publication, was written in 1857, as a Review of the Private Correspondence of DANIEL WEBSTER. It was then deemed by competent critics, "unsuited to the times," and unworthy of publication. Your admiration of the great "Defender of the Constitution" and Champion of the Union, has led you to a different conclusion. I therefore submit the manuscript to your care, only adding that your generous appreciation of my labors will ever remain among the most pleasant memories of my professional iife.

Very truly, your Friend and Teacher,

E. D. SANBORN.

REVIEW.

Eminent statesmen and jurists are seldom good letter writers. Their thoughts do not flow gracefully in the channels of social life. They are not often fluent and easy conversers. Their duties make them grave, reserved and self-reliant. It is their habit to dictate and decide, not to confer and advise. The themes of their daily meditation do not stimulate the taste, the affections and the imagination. Their thoughts are oftener occupied with the just, the useful and the expedient than with "the good, the true and the beautiful." The science of government requires depth, solidity and comprehensiveness of intellect rather than the brilliant and showy attributes of fascinating companionship. Statesmen engrossed with public cares rarely bestow much time upon the graces of epistolary correspondence or elegant conversation. From the renown of Lord Chatham as a minister of state and an orator, we should expect to find his letters abounding in wisdom and sentiment; but in the four heavy octavos edited by the Executors of his son, we look in vain for any striking display of either. About one-third of the entire work is made up of the interchange of courtly compliments between state officials. Another third is filled with partisan criticisms of men and measures, or with the formal statement of political opinions. The remaining third is occupied with personal matters of very little interest to the public. We meet with an abundance of delicate flattery, and hollow compliments; but the proofs of sincere friendship are as rare as diamonds in a desert. We are surprized to find the stout-hearted, self-sufficient premier so often "laying himself at the feet of the king." Such expressions are tolerable, perhaps, when addressed to the monarch himself, but they were not confined to such occasions. Writing to the Earl of Bute, under date of of October 8, 1761, he says,

" I have not words to express the sentiments of veneration and gratitude with which I receive the unbounded effects of beneficence and grace, which the most benign of sovereigns has condescended to bestow on me, and on those most dear to me. Your lordship will not wonder if the sensations which possess my whole breast refuse me the power of describing their extent and leave me only to beg your lordship will be so good as to lay me and Lady Hester at the king's feet and to offer for us to his Majesty the genuine tribute of the truly feeling heart, which, I will dare to hope, the same royal benevolence which showers on the unmeritorious such unlimited benefits may deign to accept with equal condescension and goodness."

No poet laureate ever dared a loftier flight in honor of his sovereign. Not even the Roman Horace, who earned his daily bread by sweet flatteries, ever expressed such unbounded gratitude to his dear Mæcenas or to his imperial patron. This was the usnal style of address from Lord Chatham to George the Third, who, at the very time when the epistle was dated, was endeavoring to silence "the great Commoner," by a peerage or a pension, and a few years afterwards, longed for the hour when "decrepitude or age should put an end to him as the trumpet of sedition." The best portion of the entire Correspondence of Lord Chatham is that which contains his letters to his nephew, while a member of the University. They were deemed worthy of publication in a separate volume in 1804. Lord Grenville, the editor of the letters, added a copious commentary of his own, generally commending the sentiments penned by Chatham, but sometimes apologizing for the advice he gives and the authors he recommends. These twenty-three letters abound in excellent sentiments upon the minor morals of College life ; but had they not been written by the foremost man of his age, they never would have been deemed above the capacity of an ordinary teacher of youth. The greatest charm about them after all is the honest affection which they exhibit. They show that the great heart of the premier beat with the same emotions which quicken the pulses of common men. For the same reason we admire the hearty outpourings of love in his letters to Lady Chatham. A brief extract from a letter dated February 22, 1766, may suffice to show what is meant :

> "Happy, indeed, was the scene of this glorious *morning* (for at half past one we divided), when the sun of liberty shone once more benignly upon a country, too long benighted. My dear love, not all the applauding joy which the hearts of animated gratitude, saved from despair and bankruptcy, uttered in the lobby, could touch me in any degree, like the tender and lively delight which breathes in your warm and affectionate note."

We find a few such oases in the wide waste of political common places ; but whoever reads the Chatham Correspondence, thinking to be warmed with the pathos and fire which characterize his speeches in favor of American freedom, will be wofully disappointed. The work is valuable to the professional man and the student of history, but possesses little interest for the common reader. The same is true of the memoirs and private correspondence of a majority of the distinguished statesmen, orators and lawyers of England. For forty years, Sir Robert Walpole was the the leading mind in the Parliament and Cabinet of Great Britain. His Memoirs, published in four huge quartos by the Rev. Wilham

Coxe, is an intensely dull and stupid work. The letters of the minister and his friends, which fill three volumes, resemble the columns of a political journal in manner and matter, except that they are not so highly seasoned with personal abuse, nor enlivened with occasional flashes of wit and satire. None but a publicist or historian would patiently wade through such a "continent of mud." Walpole's profound knowledge of men made him incapable of sincere friendship. His long and intimate acquaintance with the secret springs of political measures, made him distrust the truth of history. His biographer thus "sums up" the testimony respecting his character: "To him who directed the helm of government in England, and whose decisions affected the interests of Europe in general, all speculative opinions must have appeared dull. To him, who had drawn all his knowledge and experience from practice, all theory must have appeared trifling and erroneous. He who had fathomed the secrets of the Cabinets of Europe, must have considered history as a tissue of fables, and have smiled at the folly of those writers, who affected to penetrate into state affairs and account for all the motives of action. He who had long been the dispenser of honors and wealth, must have perceived a wide difference between the cold expressions of duty and friendship and the warm effusions of that homage which self-interest and hope inspire in those who court or expect favors. He must have been divested of human passions, had he not experienced some mortification in finding that he had been indebted to his situation for much of that obsequious regard, which he had fondly thought was paid to his personal qualities."

Who would purchase fame at such a price? Who would purchase power and place at the sacrifice of his moral nature? Walpole knew men, therefore he declared them all to be venal. It is true that his biographer modifies that far-famed assertion of his: "All men have their price," by inserting the word "*those*." "All *those* men have their price"—meaning aspirants for office, by whom he was constantly surrounded. Walpole knew how courts and camps were guided, therefore he would neither read nor hear the record of their actions. To his son, who proposed to read some historical work for his amusement, he said: "O do not read history, for that I know must be false." We admit that age, wisdom, and experience all modify the opinions of youth; but they do not necessarily lead to scepticism or misanthropy. Our own Webster served the people as long and as faithfully as Walpole did, yet he never laid aside his humanity; he never despaired of the republic, or lost his faith in a superintending Providence. Generous sentiments toward mankind, love of his native land and trust in the God of the fathers kept him hopeful and cheerful in a green old age. The speech he made, the letters he wrote, the sentiments he uttered, the prayers he offered after death had entered the very citadel of life, all testify that he died at peace with his God and with good will toward men.

The "Private Correspondence" of Mr. Webster has now been before the public for several years. It has been highly commended and bitterly assailed, like every thing else which he ever wrote or said. The political friends and enemies of the living man remain the friends and enemies of his posthumous works. When men of commanding genius are the subjects of criticism, it cannot be expected that detractors will lay aside their unreasonable prejudice, or eulogists their excessive admiration. Both classes have their successors and assigns, to whom they bequeath in trust, for coming ages, their hoarded treasures of love and hate by a testament which no litigation can annul.

A distinguished poet, artist or philosopher is often appreciated by contemporaries; always by posterity. Such men conscious of superior endowments expect immortal fame and claim it as their just reward. To those who reproached Ovid for his devotion to poetry he replied :

> " Mortale quod quæris opus; mihi fama perennis
> Quæritur ; in toto semper ut orbe canar."

Horace made a similar declaration and even boasted of the attainment of his object. Shakespeare with similar anticipations wrote to his friend :

> " Not marble nor gilded monuments
> Of princes shall outlive this powerful rhyme."

When once a favorable verdict has been pronounced on such men, their fame increases with returning years. Their defects are often forgotten ; their virtues are magnified. Each new generation rears higher the monumental pile that commemorates their greatness. Not so with the statesman. He is arraigned and tried before each successive age. He deals with questions of right and justice ; with principles which concern the dearest interests of mankind. If, like Walpole, he adopts the motto, " quieta non movere," he becomes the conspicuous target for the envenomed shafts of radicals and enthusiasts. If, like Fox, he joins the party of progress, he incurs the bitter enmity of conservatives and aristocrats. No statesman or orator of decided ability can become the favorite of the whole nation. His words divide the people as a test vote divides a legislative assembly. His opinions often conflict with those violent passions which are common to every age ; of course, they are reviewed and criticised by each succeeding race of politicians ; hence the great battles which the statesman decided for the men of his time are fought anew over his grave. His authority, when he is no more, must be put down by the same sophistry, intrigue and calumny, by which his arguments were met, while he lived. The critic who stoops to defend Lucius Sergius Catiline and Judas Iscariot hesitates not to disparage the greatest name in the annals of Rome. De Quincey assails Cicero as though he were his personal foe or some violent partisan of to-day whose influence he wished to destroy. He sets up the departed orator as a mark for his paradoxical archery ; and, with his erratic shafts steeped in opium, occasionally mars the reputation of a patriot whom sixty generations of men, with united voice, have agreed to honor. He even condescends to apologize for the ill-used victims of Ciceronian slander. "Verres," says the critic, "in the youth of Cicero, Catiline and Clodius in his middle age, Mark Antony in his old age, have all been left to operate on the modern reader's feelings precisely through that masquerade of misrepresentation which invariably accompanied the political eloquence of Rome." The gentle Catiline, forsooth, was driven to desperation by the invective of his relentless persecutor. The Roman Senators, who shunned the seat on which he sat and drowned his voice when he attempted to speak, by the universal cries of "traitor" and "parricide," were doubtless moved by unfounded prejudice. The tumults of Clodius were mere political outbreaks, like the English electioneering mobs, and these are very innocent excitements.

"We all know," says De Quincey, "that the bark of electioneering mobs is worse than their bite. Their fury is without malice, and their insurrectionary violence is without system. Most undoubtedly the mobs and seditions of Clodius are entitled to the same benefits of construction. And with regard to the graver charges against Catiline or Clodius, as men sunk irredeemably into sensual debaucheries, these are exaggerations which have told only from want of attention to Roman habits. Such charges were the standing material, the stock in trade of every orator against every antagonist. Cicero, with the same levity as every other public speaker, tossed about such atrocious libels at random."

If all that has been said of Cicero by way of commendation and censure could be collected, materials might be found among the conflicting statements for the biography of almost any conceivable character which human life presents. A philosopher or sciolist, a statesman or a demagogue, an orator or declaimer, a patriot or traitor, a hero or coward, might find, in this literary wardrobe, an appropriate dress and mask for any role he might choose to play upon the world's theatre. Those who praise and those who blame the orator derive their testimony from the same source. They find, in his letters, proofs of all the virtues that adorn the patriot and of all the vices that degrade the traitor. "No man," says Professor George Long, "can read Cicero's orations and letters without discovering that he falls far below the measure of a generous, sincere and noble character. The evidence against him is himself." If Cicero could speak to his commentator from those starry heights to which he hoped to soar, he would probably address him in the words of Charinus in the play :

> "Facile omnes, cum valemus, recta consilia ægrotis damus,
> Tu si hic sis, aliter censeas."

It is easy to be a model of consistency in your study, but difficult to be so in the turmoil of civil war. Cicero, like Webster, carved his own way to fame and rose in the popular favor by his own merit. No armed legions obeyed his call ; no trembling senate anticipated his wishes. He was a "novus homo." It was the fate of Cicero to be more bitterly maligned when dead than living. The same is true of the most illustrious of American orators. It is safe to war upon the dead. They offer no resistance. Juvenal discreetly chose, as the objects of his indignant satire, those whose ashes reposed in the Flaminian way. His example is still imitated. Men who write for effect, who cater to the worst passions of the public vainly think to elevate themselves by the exalted character of him whom they assail. To challenge a hero, even though he be dead, indicates superior prowess. It is presumptive evidence of valor to show a battered sword ; hence the doughty gladiator chooses rather to flesh his weapon in a corpse than lose the bloody sign. Even this he does, with a trembling hand and throbbing heart, all the while soliloquizing with Falstaff :

"Zounds ! I am afraid of this gunpowder Percy, though he be dead. How if he should counterfeit, too, and rise ? I am afraid he would prove the better counterfeit. I 'll make him sure : yea and I 'll swear I killed him. Why may he not rise as well as I ? Nothing confutes me but eyes, and nobody sees me. Therefore, sirrah, [stabbing him,] with a new wound in your thigh come along with me."

But Falstaff was far superior to some modern ghouls who suffer not even the grave to retain its trust. Carlyle has aptly characterized this whole race of slanderers of departed worth, in his portrait of James Heath. While the gallows was graced by the rattling bones and mouldering clay of the high-souled Oliver and his coadjutors, this royal sycophant collected and *published* all the atrocious libels which malignity and spite had invented against England's mightiest monarch. Carlyle says :

"Heath himself is called carrion-Heath as being an unfortunate, blasphemous dullard ;—blasphemous, who when he sees the image of God shining through a man, reckons it, in his sordid soul, to be the image of the devil and acts accordingly."

James Heath is the type of many a modern critic who undertakes to guide public opinion. They are known by their "furious driving," which they call "progress;" by their excessive zeal, which they call "humanity," and by their assumed infallibility, which they call "inspiration." Those who differ from them are, of course, wrong. Such men are disgusted that Mr. Webster ever achieved greatness by his genius, or gained renown by his oratory, or won affection by his virtues. They mourn daily that he ever originated a good thought, uttered a right word, or performed a worthy deed. They would gladly annihilate his fame that they may not be overshadowed by it. They think with Domitian, that by driving every good art into exile, they may reduce every thing to the dead level of their own dictation ; "ne quid usquam honestum occurreret." Whether they love or hate, they do it with their might ; and there are as many "good haters" of Daniel Webster in New England as there were of Socrates in Athens, or of Cicero in Rome But Anytus and Melitus, Clodius and Catiline were heathen, and, consequently, far less culpable for their murderous spirit, than the reckless defamers of the modern patriot, who cloak their malice under the sacred guise of philanthropy. "It requires some talent and some generosity," says an old writer, "to find out talent and generosity in others, though nothing but self-conceit and malignity are needed to discover or imagine faults." But there is little in the great and good that can die. Webster's fame is now increasing. His future life will be measured by ages ; his past by years. He still lives ; he lives in his recorded sentiments, which coming generations "will not willingly let die." He lives in his illustrious example. He lives in the gratitude and homage of all true patriots. "Vivit enim, vivetque semper; atque etiam latius in memoria hominum et sermone versabitur postquam ab oculis recessit." It is fortunate for his defamers that he has lived, otherwise they could have found no mountain sufficiently strong to resist their destructive propensities. His character furnishes a solid substratum for the practice of their oratorical gymnastics. If they do not depress him, they elevate themselves. Possibly they may do both; for it is said that a sparrow never springs from her perch without disturbing, in some degree, the motion of the earth in its orbit.

The publication of Mr. Webster's "Private Correspondence" called forth some unfriendly criticism from his political opponents, who made the vague complaint that the letters are not "equal to the prestige of the name they bear." It will be remembered that a large proportion of these letters were written in early life; many of them before he had obtained his majority; and with the exception of some of his later letters relating to questions of political interest, all were written without the most remote expectation that they would meet the public eye. Is it strange that the letters of a lad whose early advantages had been extremely limited should fall below his senatorial speeches and forensic arguments uttered under great excitement and in the full maturity of his powers? Is it strange that letters of business and friendship which were designed only to meet the wants and wishes of the hour should receive less attention than his elaborate public performances? It was never expected that the publication of these letters would add to the fame of Mr. Webster as a writer and orator; but they were issued to gratify a very laudible curiosity of his fellow citizens to become acquainted with the private life and social habits of a man so eminent as a jurist and statesman. This end they perfectly answer. They show the man as he lived and moved in society. They show how his faculties were trained and how he used them. The charm of Mr. Webster's correspondence is the *humanity* that pervades it. His familiar epistles, indited amid the pressure of higher duties, reveal his magnanimity, his generosity, his devotion to the public interests his unwavering attachment to early friends, his love of rural life and manly sports. They bind him by many new and strong ties to the common heart. They give to the people the means of forming an accurate opinion f the man whom they love to honor. The public think they have a right to know the history of their servants. Their "antecedents" are very often the source of their popularity. Farmers and mechanics are apt to look with peculiar favor upon men who rise to eminence from their own ranks. They feel that they, in some sense, are sharers in the glory thus acquired; hence there is an intense desire not only to see and hear a distinguished orator but to know how he rose to fame; to learn his genealogy and ascertain the condition and rank of his ancestors. The Roman poet assures us that a like curiosity respecting public men prevailed in his day.

"So he, who promises to guard the state,
The gods, the temples and the imperial seat,
Makes every mortal ask his father's name,
And not less curious of his mother's fame."

This desire is natural, and, if moderately indulged, is praise-worthy; but when it becomes excessive, it leads to hero-worship and meets the fate of

"Vaulting ambition, which o'erleaps itself
And falls on the other."

Mr. Webster's character will bear analysis. The severest scrutiny will find little to censure. His virtues are not dwarfed by near approach and strict examination. He was as much beloved by his personal dependants as by his warmest political admirers. Those who knew him best loved him most. His earliest friends were his latest friends. His Correspondence furnishes abundant testimony on this point. Letters addressed to the same persons in the morning and in the decline of life show that neither length of time nor distance of place had abated the warmth of his affection. Two brief extracts from his letters addressed to Mr. Bingham, whose dates are separated by nearly half a century, may suffice for an example. Under date of Feb. 22, 1803, he writes :

"MY DEAR HARVEY,

Yours of Jan. 29, was received in due season. I thank you for the expressions of friendship it contained, and for the assurance that a part of your time is devoted to me. At this period of our acquaiutance, I need not tell you what pleasnre I receive from your letters, nor with what exultation my heart glows under the impression that our early and congenial attachment will never be sundered."

After many vicissitudes of fortune on the part of his early friend, in 1849, Mr. Webster gave a favorable reply to an application from him for employment in the Department of State, introduced by the following kind and endearing allusions :

"MY DEAR OLD CLASSMATE, ROOMMATE AND FRIEND,

" It gives me very true pleasure to hear from you and to learn that you are well. Years have not abated my affectionate regard. We have been boys together, and men together, and now we are growing old together ; but you always occupy the same place in my remembrance and good wishes."

The long and intimate friendship which existed between the late Dr. Merrill and Mr. Webster is very honorable to them both. They were rivals, when students, for the highest honors of their Class ; yet, they never allowed their competition to produce the sligthest alienation between them. They corresponded for years after their graduation. In a letter addressed to the writer, dated Nov. 12, 1852, Dr. Merrill, recalling the student life of his deceased friend. says:

"As the Class gave more attention to English Branches, the latter part of the Sophomore year, and in the Junior year, Mr. Webster's character, particularly as a *writer*, and extemporaneous speaker, became developed, and he was unquestionably the best belles-lettres scholar in the Class. The fact that when a Junior, he was appointed to deliver a Fourth of July oration to the villagers shows in what estimation he was held as a writer. He, also, wrote a long Dialogue or Comedy, which required an hour or two for its recital, which the Society of which he was a member exhibited on an evening of Commencement week, at the close of his Junior year. He was altogether the best poet in the Class. He was a student of good habits. I presume confidently that he was never concerned in any mischief. I suppose he acted on the principle of mastering his lessons and attending on all ihe exercises of the College, both literary and religious."

There is in the published "Correspondence," a letter from Mr. Webster to Dr. Merrill, dated January 10, 1851, which deserves to be copied entire as an index to some of the finest traits in the character of the writer. It is as follows :

"My dear old Friend and Classmate,

"I enclose you two small recent productions, one of my lips, and one of my pen. But my purpose in writing this letter is to thank you for yours, of the 30th of July, so long unanswered, yet never forgotten. I read the "Review," both the parts marked and the parts unmarked, with much interest and satisfaction. No doubt, my dear sir, Christianity is a religion of peace; that its tendency is to put an end to wars among men, by exterminating the passions from which wars and fightings come. I assure you, my dear old Friend, that I hear from you with pleasure. You are no shepherd, and certainly I am no king. But we are friends, born in the same country, about the same age and educated at the same College. We embraced different professions, which we have pursued now for a long time, and Providence has graciously blessed us both with a great share of health and happiness. At our time of life, the mind often turns to the past. I find that I think now much more frequently than twenty or thirty years ago, on College scenes and College friends. I look over the catalogue, call to mind the dead, and inquire after the living. I well remember that I did not keep up with you in the stated course of collegiate exercises. Your lessons were better learned, and you were a great favorite with Professor Smith and other members of the authority, from the exact punctuality of all your performances. I believe I was less industrious; at any rate, I indulged more in general reading, and my attainments, if I made any, were not such as told for much in the recitation room. After leaving College, I "caught up," as the boys say, pretty well in Latin; but in College and afterwards, I left Greek to Loveland, and Mathematics to Shattuck. Would that I had pursued the Greek till I could read and understand Demosthenes in his own language!

"I shall always be happy to hear from you, my dear Sir, and hope we may, ere long, meet again, either on Otter Creek, or the Merrimac or in Marshfield.

"Your old, attached and affectionate Friend,

DANIEL WEBSTER."

Witness the *magnanimity* which concedes all that a sensitive competitor in the race of literary honors would ask, and the *modesty* which claims nothing which he would refuse. No other surviving member of the Class would have granted so much to the clergyman or withheld so much from the lawyer. The testimony of several of them is found in the volumes under review. It is unqualified with reference to the preeminence of Mr. Webster over all his classmates in every thing that constitutes liberal and comprehensive scholarship. It is, also, full and explicit with reference to his laborious habits of study, his constant devotion to duty, his cheerful obedience to law and his unblemished morality. It is fortunate that these contemporaries of his student-life survived their honored friend, to bear witness to his virtues and refute those wide spread fictions respecting his aversion to labor in boyhood, and his neglect of study in College. The record is now amended on these points and posterity will render its verdict according to the truth.

The "autobiography" which heralds the "Correspondence" is the most delightful portion of the entire work. It is a charming sketch of his early life, written for the eye of a friend. The style of this brief narrative leaves nothing to be desired. It is marked by simplicity, clearness and force. The facts are stated with that modesty which always characterizes true greatness. The autobiography and early letters furnish the best possible materials for a right estimate of Mr. Webster's character. The very fact that these letters were so carefully preserved shows that the recipients entertained even then a high opinion of the writer. They anticipated and predicted his future eminence. They witnessed the dawn of his rising reputation and hailed it with joy. Conscious of his superiority to themselves, they had the good sense to appreciate it and the generosity to admit it. They loved his social qualities, too, his large heart and gushing sympathies. Hence, they treasured up every memorial of his friendship. Many of these letters contain criticisms upon passing events and brief political disquisitions. They show that the mind of the youth was occupied with those great themes which afterwards engrossed the attention of the mature man. His College themes, his friendly letters, his newspaper essays, all reveal the "bent" of his genius and the springs of his future distinction as an orator, jurist and statesman. In the words of Tacitus : "Ingenium illustre altioribus studiis juvenis admodum dedit; non ut nomine magnifico segne otium velaret, sed quo firmior adversus fortuita Rempublicam capesseret." The family letters, too, are full of touching interest. The correspondence of the brothers, whose names are always associated, who made personal sacrifices for each other rarely equalled in the annals of fraternal love, possesses a peculiar charm for the young. These letters breathe forth the warm affections of generous souls, and reveal the manly opinions of earnest minds. They relate to a very important period in the history of the writers. They show how these young students, without the prestige of birth or the support of wealth, by the homebred virtues of industry and perseverance, forged their armor for the battle of life, and put on at the very commencement of the struggle, that invincible panoply of good habits and correct opinions, by means of which in after years, they were enabled to achieve such memorable victories. The difficulties and trials which they met and overcame are precisely the same which lie in the path of every youth who depends on his own resources for his future success. The young student, who finds the blood rushing to his heart as his eye falls on such a line as this :

"Slow rises worth by poverty depressed,"

will feel it coursing to his fingers' ends with a livelier pulsation as he reads of the conflicts and victories of these intellectual heroes in the strife. Their success will inspire hope and awaken ambition. It will do good to the soul of the desponding student "as doth a medicine." Few young men, at the present day, are subjected to severer trials of poverty than Ezekiel and Daniel Webster. A student frequenting college Halls now without a copper in his purse for a whole term, or living through the frosts and chills of a New England autumn without an overcoat, would be a "rara avis in terris." Ezekiel Webster writing to his brother under date of Nov. 6, 1802, says in conclusion :

"These cold, frosty mornings very sensibly inform me that I want a warm overcoat. I wish, Daniel, it might be convenient to send me on cloth for one; otherwise, I shall be necessitated to purchase one here. I do not care what color or what kind of cloth it is; any thing that will keep the frost out. Some kind of shaggy cloth I think would be cheapest. Deacon Pettengill has written offering me fourteen dollars a month to teach school; I believe I shall take it. MONEY, Daniel, *money!* As I was walking down to the office after a letter, I happened to find one cent, which is the only money I have had since the second day after I came on. It is a fact, Dan, that I was called on for a dollar, where I owed it, and borrowed it and have borrowed it four times since, to pay those I borrowed of.

Yours without money, E. WEBSTER.

Little thought that solitary student as he sat in his ill furnished study, with poverty "like an armed man" at his elbow dictating the message he should send to his friends at home, that men of the next generation would catch up his homely confession "to point a moral" or inspire those, "depressed" by indigence, with new courage. Little thought that younger brother, who always acted as secretary to the "committee of finance," in those family councils so often held to devise "ways and means" for replenishing their exhausted treasury, that the simple recital of their private embarrassments, would, in coming years, be read by the whole American people, aye, by the whole civilized world because of the renown of him who made the record. How it would have startled that same youth. if, while he was penning, currente calamo, those poetic effusions to his class mates, some guardian genius, in imitation of the Socratic dæmon, had whispered to his inner consciousness, that, before half a century should elapse, some astute critic would o'erlook those "hasty lines" and pronounce them unworthy of the writer's fame! We are glad that no such caveat was suggested; that no such injunction stayed his poetic essays. We can now look in upon the young orator in his hours of relaxation and see how cheerful, innocent and profitable were his amusements. All these amiable pleasantries, all the kindly greetings he sent to his young friends, all the messages whether joyous, or sad, which he sent to his almost idolized brother are irrefragable proofs of a loving heart as well as of a creative mind. They confirm the oft repeated assertion of those who knew him best, in manhood, that his affections were as remarkable as his intellect or his eloquence. Every thing animate and inanimate that reminded him of home was dear to him. The place of his birth was hallowed by a thousand precious memories. How often, in his letters and speeches, does he allude to that sacred spot and to those who there watched over his infancy and rejoiced to see his dawning fame in early manhood. Sitting in his own father's house, animated by the tender associations which three score years had thrown about it he wrote, in 1846, to Mr. Blatchford a letter full of touching pathos and pleasant reminiscences. He there said :

"Looking out at the east windows at this moment, (two P. M.) with a beautiful sun just breaking out, my eye sweeps a rich and level field of one hundred acres. At the end of it, a third of a mile off, I see plain marble gravestones designating the places where repose my father, my mother, my brother, Joseph and my sisters, Mehitable, Abigail, and Sarah, good Scripture names inherited from their Puritan ancestors. My father, Ebenezer Webster ! born at Kingston, in the lower part of the State, in 1739, and the handsomest man I ever saw, except my brother Ezekiel, who appeared to me and so does he now seem to me, the very finest human form that I ever laid eyes on. I saw him in his coffin, a white forehead, a tinged cheek, a complexion as clear as heavenly light. But where am I straying? The grave has closed upon him, as it has upon all my brothers and sisters. We shall soon be all together. But this is melancholy and I leave it. Dear, dear kindred blood, how I love you all ! This fair field is before me, I could see a lamb on any part of it. I have plowed it, and raked it, and hoed it, but I never mowed it. Somehow I could never learn to hang a scythe. I had not wit enough. My brother Joe used to say, that my father sent me to college in order to make me equal to the rest of his children!

On a hot day in July, it must have been in one of the last years of Washington's administration, I was making hay with my father just where I now see a remaining elm tree. About the middle of the afternoon the Hon. Abiel Foster, M. C. who lived in Canterbury, six miles off, called at the house, and came into the field to see my father. He was a worthy man, college learned, and had been a minister, but was not a person of any considerable natural power. My father was his friend and supporter. He talked awhile in the field, and went on his way. When he was gone, my father called me to him, and we sat down beneath the elm on a haycock. He said, My son, that is a worthy man, he is a member of Congress, he goes to Philadelphia, and gets six dollars a day, while I toil here. It is because he had an education which I never had. If I had had his early education, I should have been in Philadelphia in his place. I came near it, as it was. But I missed it and now I must work here. My dear father, said I, you shall not work. Brother and I will work for you, and wear our hands out and you shall rest. My child, said he, it is of no importance to me. I now live but for my children. I could not give your elder brothers the advantages of knowledge, but I can do something for you. Exert yourself, improve your opportunities, learn, learn, and when I am gone, you will not need to go through the hardships which I have undergone and which have made me an old man before my time.

" The next May, he took me to Exeter Phillips Academy, placed me under the tuition of its excellent preceptor, Dr. Benjamin Abbott, still living.

" My father died in April, 1806. I neither left him nor forsook him. My opening an office in Boscawen was that I might be near him. I closed his eyes in this very house. He died at sixty-seven years of age, after a life of exertion, toil and exposure; a private soldier, an officer, a legislator, a judge, every thing that a man could be, to whom learning had never disclosed her " ample page."

My first speech at the bar was made when he was on the bench. He never heard me a second time. He had in him what I collect to been the character of some of the old Puritans. He was deeply religious, but not sour. On the contrary, good-humored, facetious, showing, even in age, with a contagious laugh, teeth white as alabaster, gentle, soft, playful, and yet having a heart in him that he seemed to have borrowed from a lion. He could frown; a frown it was; but cheerfulness, good humor, and smiles composed his most usual aspect."

The characteristics, both physical and spiritual, described in this last paragraph, belonged to the son as well as to the father. This quotation, perhaps, is sufficient to indicate the strength of his affection for his father and brother. Possibly some one of the modern "captatores verborum," on reading even this, may sneeringly ask : "Is it not always to be presumed that a man loves his kindred ?" "Is it strange that a man should love his brother ?" Certainly not; nor is it strange that a man should be indifferent to his brother ; for it is not necessarily an "iron age," of which it may be said: "fratrum quoque gratia rara est." And a greater than Ovid has declared that : "A brother offended is harder to be won than a strong city ; and their contentions are like the bars of a castle." It is rare for brothers, after they attain their majority, to labor for one another, to keep a common purse and to call nothing their own. So Ezekiel and Daniel Webster loved and labored in early life. Their mutual cooperation terminated only with the death of the elder brother, whose memory the surviver ever cherished with tearful tenderness ; and in dedicating the first volume of his works to the children of that brother, he says : "I desire that the name of my brother may be associated with mine so long as any thing written or spoken by me shall be regarded or read."

Mr. Webster seemed to possess a two-fold nature. His public and private life resembled a continent divided by internal convulsions, each portion being peopled with its own race of inhabitants. In public, he appeared cold, dignified and inaccessible; in private, kind, genial and even playful. Farmers who gazed upon him with awe and reverence as he spoke at the bar or in the Senate chamber, conferred with him in private, as with an equal, and leaving his presence they exclaimed; "he is one of us." He had the rare power of entertaining persons of every age and condition with whom he happened to be associated. Mrs. E. Buckminster Lee, in a letter published in the "Private Correspondence," describing the home of Mr. Webster, at Portsmouth, says:

"After dinner, Mr. Webster would throw himself upon the sofa, and then was seen the truly electrical attraction of his character. Every person in the room was drawn immediately into his sphere; the children squeezing themselves into all possible places and posture upon the sofa in order to be close to him; Mrs. Webster sitting by his side, and the friend in the house, or social visitor, only too happy to join in the circle."

Every body knows, or pretends to know, Mr. Webster as a statesman, diplomatist and orator; but as a citizen, friend and father he has been strangely misunderstood. His letters, covering a period of more than fifty years, show more clearly than any biography can do, the true characteristics of his head and heart. Now, the very roof has been lifted from his dwelling. We can, without intrusion, look in upon him in his library or his parlor and listen to his conversation with his friends, his visitors or his children. By this process human character is tested. Addison remarks: "In private conversation with intimate friends, the wisest men very often talk like the weakest; for indeed, the talking with a friend is nothing else than thinking aloud." In his unstudied simplicity, Mr. Webster lost none of his greatness in the eyes of his domestic servants or familiar friends.

The very materials left by him, as witnesses of his whole life, show how he labored, how he thought, and how he loved. His personal habits may be detected in the amount of manuscripts left by him, and in the manner of their preservation. Every memorial of domestic endearment was carefully treasured up. The earliest scrawls of his little children, even before they were old enough to hold a steady pen or form a legible sentence, are carefully filed among the important correspondence of the year. It may be doubted whether he ever destroyed a single letter from any member of his family. His love for his children was so deep and tender, that, when they were taken from him his great heart was melted with sorrow; and for a season he was bowed to the earth with grief. Mrs. E. Buckminster Lee, describing the death of his little daughter, Grace, says :

"She awoke from a sweet sleep and asked for her father. He was instantly called, and placing his arm beneath her, he drew her towards him, when a smile of singular love and sweetness passed over her countenance and her life was gone. Mr. Webster turned away from the bed, and great tears coursed down his cheeks. I have three times seen this great man weep convulsively. Another time was when death deprived him of that brother, so tenderly loved, with whom, as we learn from the autobiography, and from his own lips, there was so close a union, that till both of them had families which drew them from each other, there had been between them but one aim, one purse, one welfare, and one hope."

After the death of his son Edward, in Mexico, Mr. Healey, the artist, executed, from daguerreotypes and other memorials of the deceased, an excellent picture of him, as he looked while living. Mr. Webster says of it, in a letter to his son : "Mr. Healey has made a most beautiful picture of dear Edward. I shall take it home and keep it before my eyes as long as I live." The same picture still hangs where the fond father placed it, in the library at Marshfield. In the busiest days of his public life, Mr. Webster usually found a few fleeting moments which he could devote to the claims of his family. He was ever ready to make any sacrifice of personal comfort to secure the happiness of the least member of his household. His thoughts of home, his domestic plans were all regulated with reference to this result. The health and prosperity of those dependent on him for employment and wages were almost daily themes of correspondence from the Senate chamber or the Department of State. When one of his laborers is reported to be ill, he writes him, with great solicitude, to guard his health, to leave labor and seek recreation, to take a journey of a few weeks and endeavor to regain his former vigor. One young man, the son of Col. Thomas, of whom he purchased the Marshfield estate, was early taken into his service and in process of time made a confidential agent in the transaction of important business in the Western States. This young man, on a visit to Washington, was seized with mortal illness. Mr. Webster left the Senate chamber and Court room to watch by his bed-side. Day and night he hung over his unquiet pillow, with all the solicitude of a father. He ministered to his bodily wants and quieted his mental excitement by words of sympathy and consolation. His attentions were gratefully acknowledged by the dying youth ; and often his rising paroxysms of insanity were soothed by falling into Mr. Webster's arms and receiving his affectionate embrace. Though alone with strangers, his mind was tranquilized when his illustrious friend was near. Mr. Webster wrote daily to his family at Marshfield of the progress of his malady ; and when he died, expressed his sorrow in most touching and pathetic language in a letter to Mrs. Webster. This warm sympathy with the suffering was a constitutional trait of his character and was strongly developed in early life. Writing to Mr. Bingham in 1803, on the death of a little sister of his friend, he says :

"Your little sister's death I hope you consider as you ought. I have no great opinion of the goodness of the heart on which such events make no impression. Innocent little thing! Thou hast been a stranger to guilt and art such to grief. Sweet be thy rest; 't is the repose of innocence. Respected be thy memory, for thou wast the sister of my friend."

Among Mr. Webster's published letters is found one addressed to Moses Davis, Esq., of Hanover, N. H., on the death of a near relative, whose acquaintance Mr. Webster made while in College. It is a model of epistolary condolence. Had it been the business of his life to visit the sick and console the mourner, he could hardly have improved its sentiments or phraseology. It was written on his twenty-second birth-day. The young student at law thus speaks of the virtues of the departed :

"During my residence in Hanover, I had more than one opportunity of witnessing the unwearied kindness of Mrs. Fuller to the sick and the necessitous. I have seen the aspect of disease brighten at her approach and sorrow and anguish banished by her tender solicitude. I have seen her house and her heart open to receive friendless strangers and to sooth and comfort the sick and forlorn. Yet however useful, human life must end. Though crowded with virtues, its date is momentary; though all be done that can be done, how little is the amount! It is the tenure by which we hold all our friends, that when He calls, whose right to them is greater than ours, we must give them up. It is the part of wisdom to think often and seriously, on the title to the good things we enjoy; and first and chiefly, to be anxious to place our happiness where vicissitudes cannot change nor accident destroy it. Low and cold and silent as your parent now is, must you and I and all our friends be. Happy, then, if we shall deserve to have shed on our graves the tears that bedew hers. I know of nothing so mortifying to the vanity of the heart, as the reflection that we must one day depart, without having our absence felt beyond the circle of a small acquaintance. Yes, it is a truth more solemn than the language it is conveyed in, that when

When you and I are gone,
The busy world will still jog on;
Will sing and dance and be as hearty
As if we still were of the party."

Little thought the youth that penned those lines, that a nation would weep over his tomb, and that "the world would feel lonely without him"!

In 1824, Mr. Webster lost a lovely boy. This affliction, for a season, almost unmanned him. When time had mellowed his sorrow, he wrote a beautiful apostrophe to that departed child. A brief quotation from the poem will indicate its character:

"I held thee on my knee, my son,
And kiss'd thee laughing, kiss'd thee weeping;
But ah! thy little day is done,
Thou 'rt with thy angel-sister sleeping.
The staff, on which my years should lean,
Is broken, ere those years come o'er me;
My funeral rite thou shouldst have seen,
But thou art in thy tomb before me.
Thou rear'st to me no filial stone,
No parent's grave with tears beholdest;
Thou art my ancestor, my son!
And stand'st in Heaven's account the oldest.
On earth, my lot was soonest cast;
Thy generation after mine;
Thou hast thy predecessor passed,
Earlier Eternity is thine."

During the last years of Mr. Webster's life, he was repeatedly called to mourn the loss of those whom he dearly loved. He often felt the need of Christian consolation while he attempted to impart it to others. After the death of his children, Major Edward Webster and Mrs. Appleton, his friends observed a settled melancholy upon his countenance. His health was manifestly affected by his poignant grief and he never, afterwards, recovered his natural buoyancy of spirits. Though his sorrow was deep and abiding, his submission to the divine will was free and cordial. To his son-in-law Mr. Samuel A. Appleton, after the death of his child, he wrote in March, 1849:

"From the first moment I heard of her illness, I had a presentiment that she would not recover. I felt that it was destined that she should immediately follow her mother.

"Bright, early, transient as the morning dew,
She sparkled, was exhaled, and went to Heaven."

"Not only on your account and that of your children, but on our own account, my dear son, this new bereavement afflicts us deeply. Every thing that is sweet, lovely and engaging in infancy, belonged to the dear little lost one. But God has seen fit to call her away and to leave us only a tender and affectionate recollection of her. I must confess that her death brings back to my heart that of her mother and seems to open afresh the fountain of tears and sorrow. Never was a daughter loved more than I loved Julia; and never was a beloved husband commiserated more than I have commiserated you. But you and I and all must submit to the will of God. We must bear these afflictions with resignation and patience, knowing that, like all other events, they are controlled and directed by unerring wisdom and goodness. What we know not now, we shall know hereafter. All is not dark and dreary, in the soul, while the lamp of religious faith and hope continues to burn. You have, yet, four beloved children about you to console and comfort you, nearer and dearer to you than to me; yet I cherish them as precious blessings to myself and as objects of affection upon whom the heart fondly leans for happy family associations and kind endearments."

What words could be more appropriate, what sentiments more consoling? What tender of paternal condolence could be better adapted to cheer the afflicted mourner and inspire hope in the soul that had been twice smitten with bereavement? What spiritual adviser who had made it the study of his life to minister consolation to the afflicted, could have presented to an enlightened faith, any stronger motives for resignation, or higher and holier sources of good hope? Such language rarely drops from the lips or flows from the pen of a man in public life.

These thoughts reveal the profound religious convictions of the writer, as well as the gushing sympathies of his loving heart. Perhaps enough has been said upon this trait of Mr. Webster's character. We pass to the brighter and more cheerful revelations of his "Private Correspondence."

Mr. Webster's idea of what epistolary correspondence, between friends, should be, may be learned not only from the general tenor of his own letters, but from his definition of it. In a letter to a classmate, in 1802, he writes :

"Correspondence is a kind of commerce where the greatest gain per cent. uniformly attaches to the greatest capital ; and there is as much to be learned in writing a good letter as in reading."

He wrote in accordance with this notion. All his early letters, even when he aims only to indite harmless pleasantries, contain some useful sentiments that render them valuable to the thoughtful. Like the true poet, he always mingled the useful with the agreeable, hence his letters are eminently instructive. Writing to the Hon. Warren Dutton, in May, 1830, he says :

"I thank you for your favor of April 19. To receive a letter at Washington, that says nothing of business, little of politics and gives a little honest Boston talk, such as the writer and the reader might hold together, if they were taking a turn in the Mall, is quite refreshing. In general, when I open a letter, the silent question which I put to myself is, who is this that wants a cadetship, a midshipman's warrant, or an errand done at one of the Departments."

This extract shows clearly how much he coveted unselfish companionship and may serve as a key to solve the standing ænigma of his life, the choice of his confidential friends. He highly prized those who loved his personal qualities more than his personal influence. A truly great man, who has political favors to bestow, can rarely find sincere friends. They are generally summer companions, basking in the sunshine of prosperity and flying when winter storms come on ;

> —— "diffugiunt cadis
> Cum fæce siccatis amici
> Ferre jugum pariter dolosi ;"

which is very happily paraphrased by Douglas Jerrold : "Friends, like tumblers in frosty weather, are apt to fly at the first touch of hot water." The same thought finds fit expression only in Shakespeare's noble measures :

> "When fortune, in her shift and change of mood,
> Spurns down her late beloved, all his dependants,
> Which labored hard after him to the mountain's top,
> Even on their knees and hands, let him slip down,
> No one accompanying his declining foot."

A statesman's friends adhere to him so long as his favor can bestow promotion. Knowing human nature thoroughly, it is not wonderful that Mr. Webster was most attached to those men who loved him on his own account, and not for the offices which his influence could secure for them. It is perfectly natural, too, that, living for years in the turmoil of political strife, he should become weary of the discussion of public measures and turn with eager delight to more welcome themes. Well informed scholars he was pleased to meet. Their society he coveted and enjoyed. Writing to Mr. Blatchford in 1849, he remarks of Mr. J. C. Gray :

"I hardly know a man of greater extent and variety of knowledge. When he is with us, I feel that I am near a great treasury of information. I can open the door at any time. How pleasant it is to be with people that can tell you something. To me, who know nothing but some law and a little politics, it is refreshing and delightful to converse with a man who has read largely and variously, who appreciates the value of what he has learned, and whose conversation running freely and naturally, like a brook from a clear spring, is neither pedantic, dogmatical nor ostentatious. This is the true flow of soul which Pope says he learned from Bolingbroke :

"Taught by thy converse happily to steer
From grave to gay, from lively to severe."

This style of conversation Mr. Webster loved in others and exhibited himself. All who knew him will readily testify that he oftener imparted than received instruction in social intercourse. His letters of friendship are full of useful information. He frequently discourses of history, geography and philosophy like one whose life had been given to those studies. The habit of defining and explaining terms sometimes appears in his epistles where you would least expect it. The illustrations used were always suggested by his subject. In a letter to a friend from Marshfield, in December, 1847, he said :

"I hear the sea very strong and low from the North, which is not unusual after violent atmospheric agitations, and when the wind has lulled. They call it the "rote" or "rut" of the sea. Either expression is correct. The Latin "rota" is the root of both words. The rut in the road is the result of rolling or the repeated and occasional pressure or blows of the wheel. Rotation means repetition as well as succession. To learn a thing by rote is to possess the mind of it by repeated readings or hearings. The rote or rut of the sea, therefore, means only the noise produced by the action of the surf, the successive breaking of wave after wave upon the shore, and the beach means precisely the smooth shore beaten by the eternal restlessness of the ocean.'

Such specimens of etymological interpretations are quite common in his letters, and were still oftener introduced in private conversation with friends. Occasionally he tries his hand at Americanisms or other anomalous expressions for the amusement of his correspondent. The following occurs in a letter written in 1850 ;

"If you think that this matter will give you any trouble, pray let me take it upon myself to *wriggle* through it. Like many other Yankees, I am apt enough to fall into difficulties, but like them, have sometimes a *knack* of *squirming* out of them. Now, write it upon your tablets that *wriggle*, *knack*, and *squirm* are lawful English words."

In addressing intimate friends he was sometimes humorous though never trifling. A letter written amid the pressure of grave matters of State, in 1842, was evidently designed as a species of burlesque on diplomatic intercourse. It is superscribed under the envelope, "For Mrs. Curtis and positively confidential and of great importance." He then gradually and cautiously reveals his secret :

"I have to communicate to you a matter of considerable importance and of a public nature, though private interests and wishes are connected with it. It is not that "a couple of treaties" were signed, as report says, yesterday, in my Department, nor that the President sent on the same day, a greater or less number of vetoes to Congress ; the President likes a good many vetoes. The matter I have to communicate, though of a public nature, is yet a profound secret. My wife does not know a word about it ; or rather, I have not told her a word ; but I dare say she knows all about it. Strong sympathies, a sort of matrimonial magnetism, enables her to find out what I know, without the use of speech. By the way, she is very well and bright. If you, who always thought her a great beauty, were to see her now, you would agree that she has still further improved. She will be going North in about ten days ; and if you are in New York, she will be happy to see you. But I stay you from my subject. What I have to say does not respect any pending negotiation, spun out like a Spanish war, but which, like a Spanish war, at length came to an end. But I must hasten to announce the news ; and it is time I should, for I hate all useless preliminary flourishing of words. In res medias ; to hasten into the middle of a matter is a rule in poetry, oratory, history, and other matters. Well, then, here it comes. I may as well begin to state it now, or else I shall be driven to a second sheet and paper is scarce. I am already near the bottom of the second page. I will reveal the whole at once. Two days before the last anniversary of American Independence, being the sixty-sixth (I believe) on the second day of July last, there was regularly passed a DOCUMENT, C. H. of Vermont was made a middie" ! ! !

Whatever might be his mood of thought, whether grave or gay, he always made an effort to impart it to his correspondent ; hence his letters, like daguerreotypes, give us true pictures of his daily reflections. Writing, with him, was a substitute for conversation. His theme is usually suggested by the circumstances that surround him. Geography, natural history, rural scenery, agriculture and local associations employed his pen more than literary or political topics. Writing from the old homestead, in 1849, he says :

"This place looks charmingly. It is the delight of my eyes to behold. Some of the crops were short ; but the rain has renewed every thing and this beautiful meadow before me seems the sweetest spot on earth, verdant and smiling as it is and surrounded by high hills. It was the view of some such place as this that Dr. Watts spiritualized :

"A little spot enclosed by grace,
From out the world's wide wilderness."

In another letter to the same friend, written in the same room, in 1850, he says :

"This castle has a pleasant seat ; the air
Nimbly and sweetly recommends itself unto
Our gentle senses.

"Throw physic to the dogs — I'll none of it ;
Nor rhubarb, senna, nor a purgative drug."

But Dunsinane was a foggy, sickly spot compared with Elms Farm, nor did Scotland ever see such a forest prospect as the sun at this moment begins to shine upon. The row of maples by the side of my field for half a mile, shows a broad line of burnished gold ; and the side hill west of the house displays every possible variety of tint, from the deepest and darkest evergreen to the brightest orange. It seems to me the finest morning I ever saw. Chips enough and by the looks of John Taylor's larder, we can laugh a siege to scorn."

These extracts indicate that the associations of time and place always furnished materials for thought. Whether he floated upon the ocean, travelled by land, or looked out, from the windows of his hotel, upon the spires and roofs of an ancient city, the impressions he received were embodied in his letters. In 1847 he made a journey through several of the Southern States. From every stopping place, he sent back his new thoughts to his friends at home. Hours which others gave to sleep, he devoted to correspondents. Some of the most beautiful sentiments he ever penned were inspired by the hour when they were written. Such is that oft-quoted description of the morning addressed to Mrs. Paige, from the city of Richmond. A single paragraph will show what is meant :

" Beautiful descriptions of the " morning" abound in all languages but they are strongest, perhaps, in those of the East, where the sun is so often an object of worship. King David speaks of taking to himself " the wings of the morning." This is highly poetical and beautiful. " The wings of the morning" are the beams of the rising sun. Rays of light are wings. It is thus said that the Sun of Righteousness shall arise " with healing in his wings ;" a rising sun which shall scatter light and health, and joy throughout the universe. Milton has fine descriptions of morning, but not so many as Shakespeare, from whose writings pages of the most beautiful images, all founded on the glory of the morning might be filled."

By way of contrast to this poetic description, addressed to a lady who would appreciate and enjoy it, I will quote a passage written during the same tour, from Charleston to Mr. Weston, a practical mechanic of Marshfield. He says :

" In North Carolina we travelled two hundred miles in the tar and turpentine country. The pine from which these are obtained is the long leaved pine, a good deal resembling our pitch pine but much fuller of sap. They make a notch in the tree called a " box," and cut the bark off a foot above it. The turpentine runs down into this " box" and when the box gets full they ladle it out. A box holds a quart and will fill three or five times in the season. A handsome tree with " boxes" will yield ten quarts a year. Tar is made by burning pine knots, stumps, &c., in a pit like charcoal. The sap sweats out and runs into a hole prepared for it in the ground. One barrel of turpentine distilled makes six gallons of spirit. The residuum, or resin is not of much value, say twenty-five cents a barrel."

In the same letter he describes the process of raising rice and makes it so plain that no person who reads can mistake his meaning. When Mr. Webster travelled for recreation, he banished all thoughts of business. He followed literally the advice of Horace to Torquatus :

"Then instant from the busy world retire,
And, while your tedious clients fill the hall,
Slip out at the back door and bilk them all.

On such occasions the common thoroughfares and places of popular resort had no charms for him. A crowd interrupted his free communion with nature. From Sterling, in Scotland, in 1839, he writes :

"We have passed rather rapidly through some of the lake scenery of Scotland. Many have seen this and many have described it. Since Walter Scott's Lady of the Lake, all have felt a new interest in this part of Scotland; and now, since steamboats are on every lake and river, where there is water enough to float them, crowds follow crowds through the whole travelling season, all along the common track. This takes off much of the romance and much of the interest. We travel together and every body is in a prodigious hurry. The inns are all thronged ; the carriages are crammed and the decks of steamboats crowded with a mass of men and women, each with a guide book in hand learning what to admire ! The scenery, in itself, is truly beautiful and I have learned enough to know, I think, how one should travel in order to enjoy it, the great majority of the travellers only wish "*to get on.*" Their first inquiry is, how soon they can get to a place ; the next, how soon they can get away from it. They incur the expense of the journey for the sake of having the power of saying afterwards that they have seen sights, more than from any other motive. If I could go through this lake region, at leisure, and with one friend of discernment, taste and feeling, I should experience, I am sure, the greatest possible delight."

Mr. Webster's careful preparation for travel is evinced in the multitude of maps and works descriptive of the countries he visited, which are now found in his library at Marshfield. It was his custom to examine carefully the geography and local history of a town, city, or country before he visited it ; and when he was passing through it, or resting in it, he observed its physical features with the eye of a landscape painter and noted the customs and morals of the place with the nice discrimination of a philosopher. The results of his observation and reflection constitute the chief materials of his letters to his friends. This habit of accurate investigation gave a peculiar charm to his "Private Correspondence." It imparted beauty and perspicuity to his descriptions, and when applied to arguments, rendered his logic irresistible. The clearness and accuracy of his statements often gave to the deductions of his reason the force of demonstration. This mental habit was the result of severe discipline, early commenced and faithfully practised. More than fifty years ago, writing to a College friend respecting the desultory habit of reading history, formed by students, he said:

"We often read page after page and retain only a slender thread of events, every thing else gliding from the memory about as fast as the the eye traces the lines of the book. Yet when we examine a particular occurrence or search after a single date, the impression is permanent and we have added an idea to the stock of our knowledge."

The habit of reading history with the map of the countries described open before the reader and the necessity of ascertaining the relative position of different provinces and the exact location where important events took place is frequently inculcated upon his children in his familiar letters to them. His method of reading, while a student, is thus described to a classmate:

"So much as I read, I made my own. When a half hour or an hour at most had expired I closed my book and thought it all over. If there was anything particularly interesting to me, either in sentiment or language, I endeavored to recall it and lay it up in memory and commonly could effect my object."

Such careful reading must inevitably give certainty to knowledge, force to argument and perspicuity to style. Mr. Webster's manuscripts give us the results of his researches; his library shows us where he has travelled in the realms of mind; and where he tarried but for a night, you discover traces of his industry. Previous to the year 1840, he had occasion to learn the physical and political condition of New Zealand. Every important work that had then been published relative to that island, from the voyages of Capt. Cook to the latest missionaay report, was purchased for consultation. This is but a single instance of his multiplying works of reference. In his agricultural researches, he procured and consulted the best authorities in every department of natural history and the useful arts. The animal kingdom, in all its varieties, arrested his attention, employed his leisure hours and enriched his mind. Proofs of these researches are found in numerous letters of the "Correspondence." The habits of fishes and birds are frequently described in his letters. The good points of every species of domestic animal were as familiar to him as the countenances of men, and these, too, often employed his pen. When in England, he observed with more care the fields and flocks than the Court and the Parliament. Writing from London, under date of Sept. 20, 1839, he says :

"Within the first six weeks we have run over much of England and some of Scotland. Of course, we could stay but a little time in any place, nor were we able to see much below the surface of things. But the agriculture in England and Scotland, I have looked at pretty attentively. Taken altogether, England exhibits a high wrought, exact, elaborate system of art and industry. Every productive power is carried to the utmost extent of skill and maintained in the most unceasing activity. Constant attention and close calculation pervade every thing. Rent is high, but the prices of produce are high also. About thirty shillings sterling, say seven dollars, may be regarded, perhaps, as near the average rent of good land in England. In some parts, it is much higher, say ten dollars, or rent and tithes together, fifteen. The land is mostly productive and prices are high. A gentleman told me, yesterday, that he had sold, some weeks ago, his wheat crop at eleven pounds sterling per acre, standing, and his oat crop for eight. This will show you the aggregate of products and prices. Forty bushels of wheat and fifty or even sixty of oats are not an uncommon yield to the acre. The land is naturally good and is subjected to the most careful and skillful cultivation. Iu tha course ef forty years, the *turnip* has vastly enriched England. It feeds millions of sheep, whose wool and flesh command high prices ; and feeding them in the fields during the winter, say ten sheep to the acre, enriehes the land for a succeeding crop of wheat. Then, too, lime is used extensively and every bone is ground up for bone dust, which is found a most powerful manure, and when the lands require it, a complete system of underdraining, especially in Scotland, is adopted, which produces the best results. Agricultural labor is not more than half as dear in England as in the United States."

It would be impossible, within the bounds of a brief review, to illustrate the extent and variety of Mr. Webster's epistolary compositions. There is scarcely a topic of human interest that he has not discussed in his letters, from the humblest employments of daily life to the sublimest themes of our holy religion. He never wrote in vain. We do not pretend that he always writes profoundly or learnedly upon every subject. No man is great in every department of labor or study. Few excel in more than one. We should not look for belles-lettres scholars in Ministers of State or in great warriors. Such men make history, they cannot stay to write it, much less to frame honied sentences for ears polite, or iudite pleasant epistles to charm the hearts of admiring friends. Cæsar was an exception. His stylus was as keen as his sword. His intellect was as polished as his armor. His "Commentaries" are as brilliant and impressive as his victories. Still his "veni, vidi, vici" reveals the condensation of his thoughts as much as it does the rapidity of his marches. Bonaparte's epistles resemble telegraphic communications, and his speeches, too, were marked by the same terseness, point and brevity. The "Iron Duke" was as laconic in his dispatches as he was resistless in the field. "Great commanders," said Montesquieu, "record their actions with simplicity, for they have more glory from deeds than from words." Orators, whose vocation embraces a larger variety of topics, usually exhibit greater versatility of thought in their compositions. We sometimes meet with one, like Burke, who has a vein of the "sublime and beautiful" in the molten gold which flows, ore rotundo, from his intellectual crucible. Another, like Brougham, writes learnedly upon all themes, but attains the "aliquid immensum infinitumque" in none. A third, like Canning, excels in political satire and biting sarcasm, and surpasses Juvenal in the flow of his verse and pungency of his wit. Another, like Webster, would, at his own fireside, utter in the ear of friendship "thoughts that breathe and words that burn," whose tones, caught up by the press, would warm and cheer the heart of a nation ; or sitting in his library at Marshfield, would indite an epistle whose beautiful sentiments would, like England's martial strains, soon encircle the globe. It deserves notice that Mr. Webster perpetuates no feuds. His writings cannot be used for partisan purposes. If he had prejudices against other statesmen, he has not incorporated them into his letters. He seldom alludes to public men but to commend them. If he could not speak kindly of them he was silent. He has, therefore, left no wrongs to be redressed, no personal controversies to be adopted by his friends. From his letters alone, we should scarcely know that he had political opponents. No trace of bitterness or vindictiveness mars a single page of his correspondence. There were men, (in his native State, too,) who dogged his steps with libels for more than thirty years, whom he kindly forgave and who, during the last years of his life, enjoyed his generous hospitality, at the old homestead, in Franklin. In some instances during his long public life, he employed in his speeches, usually in self-defence, the strong language of invective. When his speeches were published, he desired the editor to obliterate from them all traces of unkindness and severity. His words were :

"My friend, I wish to perpetuate no feuds. I have lived a life of strenuous political warfare. I have sometimes, though rarely, and that in self-defence, been led to speak of others with severity. I beg you, when you can do it without wholly changing the character of the speech, and thus doing essential injustice to me, to obliterate every trace of personality of this kind. I should prefer not to leave a word that would give unnecessary pain, to any honest man, however opposed to me."

Happy would it have been for the world, if all the distinguished men of past ages had taken similar precaution. Mr. Webster carried this same regard for the feelings of others into social life, and where he had, in the heat of controversy, betrayed any undue excitement, he, with singular magnanimity, made advances toward a reconciliation. The following brief note to Mr. Blatchford explains itself :

WASHINGTON, JAN. 2, 1849.

DEAR SIR,

You are acquainted with a little occurrence which took place here last year between Mr. Ogden and myself. Mr. Ogden took offence at a remark which I felt it my duty to make to the Court, and has not called to see me since, when I have been in New York, as used to be his friendly habit. I do not like that any coldness should exist between myself and a gentleman with whom I have been long on friendly terms, unless such be his pleasure. The occasion has passed by ; I feel no unkindness towards Mr. Ogden. I have eaten bread and tasted wine at his hospitable table, in times long since past. I have never lost, and shall not lose, a just appreciation of his character, professional and personal, and shall always be far more willing to show kindness than to do injury to him or his friends.

You may show this to Mr. Hall, and if you and he think proper, he may suggest the contents of it to Mr. Ogden. My real motive in this is, that if Mr. Ogden feels any degree of unhappiness at what has occurred, he may dismiss it from his mind.

Yours, truly, always,

DANIEL WEBSTER.

The letters which were exchanged between Mr. Webster and the Hon. D. S. Dickinson, near the close of the year 1850, are of the same import. These gentlemen had been, for many years, warm political opponents and had sometimes pointedly assailed each other, so as to leave behind the sting of reproof. Mr. Webster offered terms of peace with dignified condescension. Mr. Dickinson received them with generous alacrity. He says of Mr. Webster's letter :

" Numerous and valued are the testimonials of confidence and regard which a somewhat extended acquaintance and lengthened public service have gathered round me, but, amongst them all, there is none to which my heart clings so fondly as this. I have presented it to my family and friends as the proudest passage in the history of my eventful life, and shall transmit it to my posterity as a sacred and cherished memento of friendship."

Other testimonials to Mr. Webster's magnanimity and Christian courtesy exist among his unpublished correspondence. In due time, when the seal of privacy shall have been broken, they will come forth to give new lustre to the last days of his public life. Such a kind and conciliatory temper is not the product of wounded sensibility or disappointed ambition ; nor is it the legitimate fruit of declining years. The poetic view of old age is not a pleasing one. Horace thus characterizes it :

" Difficilis, querulus, laudator temporis acti
Se puero."

Juvenal is positively ferocious in his description

of its complaining helplessness and disgusting dotage. The English imitators of these satirists, with the aids of Christian culture, have obliterated none of the dark colors from these ancient pictures of decaying manhood. We expect, therefore, that increasing years will strengthen the "ruling passion" of early life. For this reason, the exhibition of a forgiving spirit compels us to admit the existence of those Christian graces in which it has its origin.

Partisan critics have searched the "Private Correspondence" of Mr. Webster, with the keen vision of "an eagle or Epidaurian serpent" for proofs of vanity, prejudice, or despondency, such as are found in the letters of Cicero ; but not a solitary instance rewards their toil. They find instead, reverence for law and religion, warm patriotism and undying love of liberty. The religious press quotes from Mr. Webster's Correspondence, as the most weighty authority they can cite, when his opinions accord with their own. Sometimes, by a species of pious fraud, a forged letter is extensively circulated for the good of the cause; but when the same press speaks of Mr. Webster's character and principles, they adopt, with apparent respect, the slanderous words of one who classes the Holy Scriptures with the Shaster and Zendavesta, and ranks the inspiration of John, "the beloved disciple," and "Paul the aged," with that of Homer, Milton and Shakespeare. Sometimes an "untravelled" pastor treats the "fall of Adam" and the fall of Webster in the same discourse, seeming to place the "apostacy" of the latter in the same category with that of the former ; and, to make the words of inspiration doubly significant to those who aspire to be as gods, either in knowledge or power, declares that "the greatest of American statesmen died of a broken heart, because he could not obtain the presidency of the United States." Both the physicians who attended him in his last illness, and the "candid public" entertain a different opinion with reference to the cause of his death. To those who are disposed to call in question Mr. Webster's patriotism or philanthropy, we commend the reading of his "Private Correspondence." On every page of that work, we find that the spring of all his actions was a great and loving heart. From youth to age, he sought his country's welfare. With the utmost sincerity, he might have adopted the words of Milton :

" While I was yet a child, no childish play
To me was pleasing; all my mind was set,
Serious, to learn and know and thence to do
What might be PUBLIC GOOD ; myself I thought
Born to that end ; born to promote all truth."

During the last year of Mr. Webster's senatorial life, questions of great importance came before Congress. He chose his position after mature deliberation and from profound conviction of its rectitude. His motives have been assailed, his character traduced and his reputation blackened, by men who claim the largest liberty of opinion, but allow no man to differ, with impunity, from themselves. Until Mr. Webster's veracity shall have been successfully impeached, by showing that, in every speech he ever made and in every deed he ever performed, he was then and there enacting and uttering falsehood, it is proper to allow him to testify in his own case and to give him credit for the same candor and honesty which have been conceded to him in all other cases. In a letter addressed to Messrs. Richards and others, dated March 21, 1851, he thus explains his action in that crisis :

"If I have attempted to expound the Constitution, I have attempted to expound that which I have studied with diligence and veneration from my early manhood to the present day. If I have endeavored to defend and uphold the Union of the States, it is because my fixed judgment and my unalterable affections have impelled me, and still impel me, to regard that Union as the only security for general prosperity and national glory. * * * * * * * * *
I was not unaware, gentlemen, on the morning of the 7th of March last year, that I was entering upon a duty which, as you suggest, might bring into peril that favor which has so long been shown me by that political party whose general principles I had for a long time steadily maintained. A crisis had arrived, in which it did not become me, as I thought, to be indifferent and do nothing. Still less did it become me to act a part which should inflame sectional animosities, and tend to destroy all genuine American feeling, and shake the fabric of the government to its foundations. I was willing to trust and am still willing to trust for the vindication of my motives, to the intelligent men of my party and of all parties. I should, indeed, have been wholly unworthy of that character, which it is my highest ambition to maintain among my countrymen, if I had allowed any personal peril to bear with the weight of a feather against my profound sense of public duty. Whatever may now happen, I shall meet it with a clear conscience, and a fixed purpose, and while acting in full coöperation with the great mass of our fellow citizens, who hold the same sentiments that you hold, I shall fear nothing."

This declaration, recorded with such solemnity of tone and language, ought to secure for the opinions of the writer, toleration, if not approbation. Certainly it ought forever to silence the charges of insincerity and hostility to liberty. It is true that many of Mr. Webster's political friends were alienated by the course he pursued with reference to the Compromise measures. This was not the first instance in his long public life when his supporters deserted him. He was more fiercely assailed by his party than by his opponents for remaining in President Tyler's Cabinet to adjust the North Eastern boundary question. Many of his old friends attacked him through the press ; others poured upon him their remonstrances in numerous letters, making passionate appeals to his self-respect, his love of a good name, and his habitual integrity. Such assaults were more difficult to be repelled than those of open enemies. But he remained true to himself, and to his country. He understood the importance of the crisis and the necessity that Providence had laid upon him to rescue his country from impending war. He resolved to meet the storm of obloquy from friends and foes and trust to truth and time for a vindication of his course. He succeeded and all the interested parties now commend his wisdom. Down to the last hour of this harrassing and laborious negotiation, men who had formerly cooperated with him and even received at his hand essential aid in their own promotion, charged him with love of power and ambition in retaining his place. These unfounded accusations added to the exhausting labors of the Department of State "drank up" his spirits and wasted his strength. His friend, George W. Nesmith, Esq. says in a letter to the writer that Mr. Webster informed him,

"That during the time he was engaged in making the Ashburton Treaty, he was so constantly employed, that he did not sleep more than three hours, each night, for three months together ; and that he had still less undisturbed repose for five months in succession during the exciting discussions of 1850."

This fact indicates, on both occasions, unwearied diligence and constant solicitude. The distinguished diplomatists representing the high contracting parties to the Washington Treaty formed for each other a sincere and lasting friendship. Lord Ashburton and Mr. Webster maintained till the death of one of the parties, an affectionate and confidential correspondence. It deserves a passing notice that this treaty met with decided opposition in England as well as in the United States; and both the diplomatists were severely censured, at home, for surrendering valuable national claims; but the murmurs of disaffected partisans were soon drowned by the general acclamations of the friends of peace in both nations. A similar change of feeling might have been anticipated with regard to Mr. Webster's course in the Senate in 1850, had he lived to interpret and enforce his published opinions. His bitterest opponents admit that his presence in the Senate would, undoubtedly, have have prevented the hasty and ill-considered legislation which, since his decease, has brought the country to the verge of civil war.* If Hector had not fallen, there would have been no occasion for the mournful strains of the poet:

> ——— "Fuimus Troes; fuit Ilium et ingens
> Gloria Teucrorum."

However, it is not an unheard of thing, that an aged statesman, when his large experience and mature wisdom are of most value to his countrymen, should lose the support or incur the displeasure of his former friends. Pericles, whose dying boast it was, that no Athenian had ever worn mourning through his agency, found his last days embittered by the unreasonable hostility of his fellow citizens. Demosthenes escaped a public execution by suicide. Cicero fell by the knife of a hired assassin and his head graced the very rostrum from which he had so often defended his ungrateful country. Pitt, "the greatest minister of his century, one of the very few great men of his age, among orators the only peer of Demosthenes, the man without title or fortune,

* This Review was written before the war.

who, finding England in the abyss of weakness and disgrace, conquered Canada, and the Ohio valley, and Gaudaloupe, humbled France, gained the dominion of the seas, won the supremacy in Hindostan, and, at home, vanquished faction," on the accession of a new monarch, was compelled to resign the seals of office and allow ordinary men to wear his laurels. Burke spent the leisure of his old age in refuting the theories of his youth. Wellington closed the windows of his palace with iron shutters to exclude the missiles of that very populace, in the capital, that had so often rent the air with shouts in honor of the hero of Waterloo! Webster was shut out from Faneuil Hall by the magistrates of the city of his adoption, which owed to his eloquence her commercial prosperity, and of which himself was the brightest ornament. But no one of these statesmen is less honored now, because the ship of State, while he guided its helm, encountered adverse winds and storms. The fame of Webster is still dear to the American people. The publication of his "Private Correspondence" has made the people better acquainted with the amiable traits of his character. "Real virtue," says Plutarch, "is most beloved, when it is most nearly seen; and no respect which it commands from strangers can equal the never ceasing admiration it excites in the daily intercourse of domestic life."

www.ingramcontent.com/pod-product-compliance
Lightning Source LLC
LaVergne TN
LVHW011121110826
845150LV00008B/2211
9781418198077